ECIA CHAPTER II F.X.

PROPERTY OF
ST. CLEMENT'S
LIBRARY
ROSEDALE, MD.

VALORIE GRIGOLI

PATRIOTIC HOLIDAYS AND CELEBRATIONS

FRANKLIN WATTS
New York / London / Toronto / Sydney / 1985
A FIRST BOOK

FOR MY MOTHER AND FATHER

Photographs courtesy of:
UPI/Bettmann Newsphotos: opposite p. 1,
pp. 10, 13, 14, 56, 57;
Yale University Art Gallery: p. 6;
United Nations/Y. Nagata: p. 23;
The Metropolitan Museum of Art,
Gift of John S. Kennedy, 1897: p. 30;
Library of Congress: p. 33;
Pictorial Parade: p. 37;
The Metropolitan Museum of Art,
Gift of J. Pierpont Morgan, 1900: p. 41;
Paul Thompson/European Picture Service: p. 47.

Library of Congress Cataloging in Publication Data

Grigoli, Valorie.
Patriotic holidays and celebrations.

(A First book)
Includes index.
Summary: Examines patriotic holidays in America, including national holidays such as Independence Day, regional celebrations such as the Cheyenne Frontier Days, military holidays, and those associated with individuals.
1. Holidays—United States—Juvenile literature.
2. Patriotism—United States—Juvenile literature.
[1. Holidays. 2. Patriotism] I. Title.
JK1761.G75 1985   394.2'684'73   85-7270
ISBN 0-531-10044-8

Copyright © 1985 by Valorie Grigoli
All rights reserved
Printed in the United States of America
5 4 3

CONTENTS

INTRODUCTION
1

BUILDING A NATION
3

Independence Day
Labor Day
Inauguration Day
Pan American Day
Flag Day
Citizenship Day
United Nations Day
General Election Day
Bill of Rights Day

PEOPLE AND PERSONALITIES
28

Presidents' Day
George Washington's Birthday
Abraham Lincoln's Birthday
Martin Luther King, Jr., Day
Columbus Day

MILITARY HOLIDAYS
43

Memorial Day
Veterans' Day
Armed Forces Day

SOME REGIONAL HOLIDAYS AND CELEBRATIONS
52

Arbor Day
Saint Paul Winter Carnival
Patriots' Day
Confederate Memorial Day
Cinco de Mayo
Cheyenne Frontier Days
American Indian Day

PATRIOTISM ALL YEAR 'ROUND
63

INDEX
65

PATRIOTIC HOLIDAYS AND CELEBRATIONS

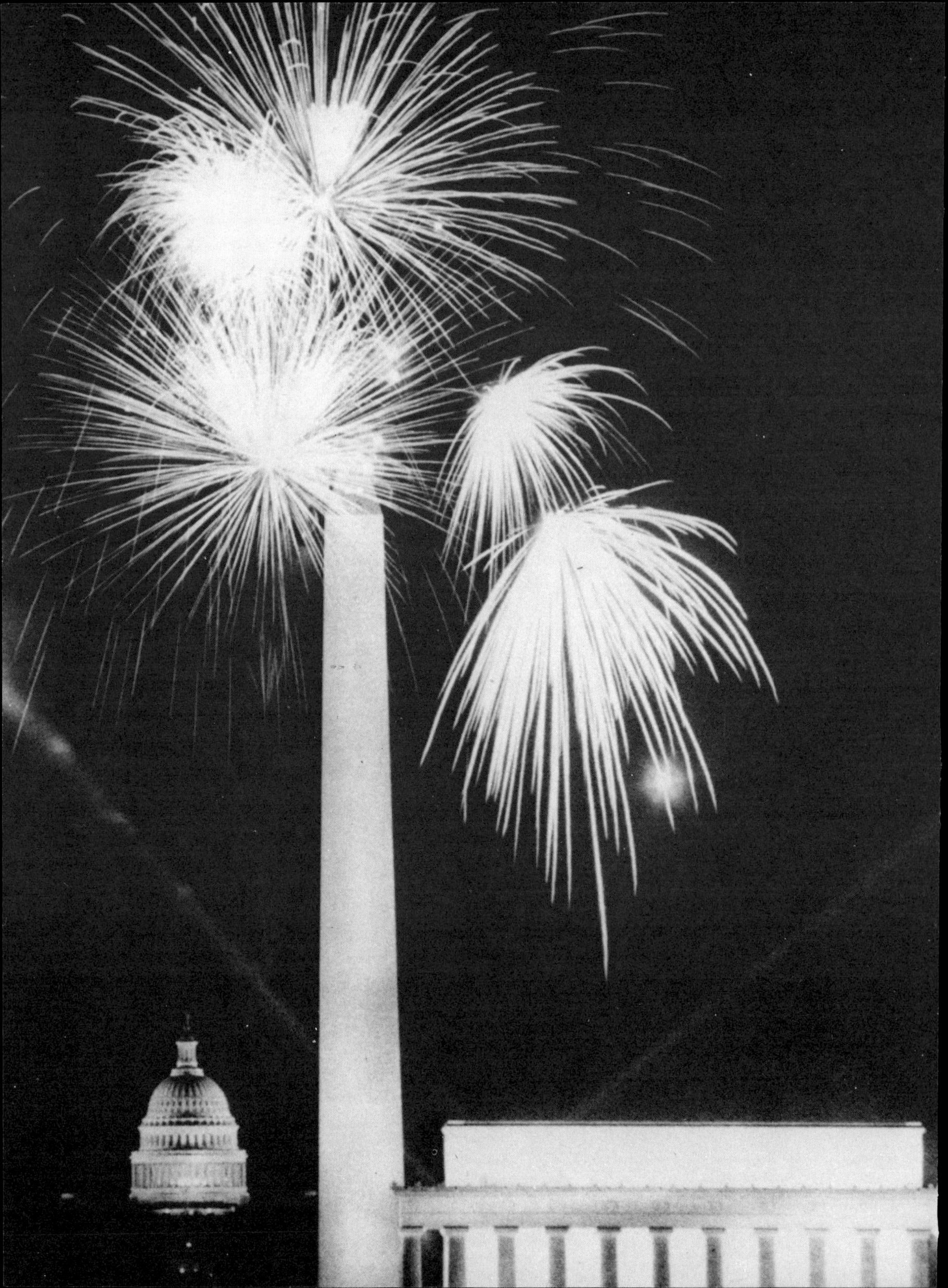

INTRODUCTION

Are you patriotic? You are if you love your country. You show your patriotism in many ways: by singing "The Star Spangled Banner," or by saying the Pledge of Allegiance to the flag. You show patriotism when you cheer as a military parade passes by or thrill to a fireworks display on the Fourth of July.

The mid-1980s is a time of especially great patriotism in America. The United States won more gold medals than any other country in the 1984 Olympics, and Americans were very proud. President Reagan's campaign for re-election stressed patriotism.

Another clue to just how patriotic we are is the great number of patriotic holidays and celebrations we have. We Americans love our country, and we show it by celebrating. In this book we are going to learn about all kinds of patriotic holidays and celebrations. We'll look at national patriotic holidays, such as Independence Day and Memorial Day, which are celebrated by all American citizens. We'll look at patriotic holidays set aside by presidential proclamation. While you may not get to stay home from school on these days, such holidays as Armed Forces Day and Flag Day are very important.

We'll also "travel" to different parts of the country to sample a few of the thousands of regional patriotic celebrations and holidays. You might find your own state or region represented in the section of this book called "Some Regional Holidays and Celebrations."

Along the way you'll learn a lot about the events and the people who shaped our country. You'll also find activities and ideas for your own celebrations, from grand, big-city festivals to small-town shindigs. Here we go!

1
BUILDING A NATION

There are two national holidays of a patriotic nature that every state in the country observes—Independence Day and Labor Day. In addition, there are numerous special days in which we hold elections or simply recognize an important historic event.

INDEPENDENCE DAY

It's fitting that we should begin with our most important national holiday—our country's birthday! Independence Day, the Fourth of July, is the day that the American colonies adopted the Declaration of Independence, declaring themselves independent from England and the rule of King George III.

> We hold these truths to be self-evident, that all men are created equal, that they are endowed by their Creator with certain unalienable rights, that among these are Life, Liberty, and the Pursuit of Happiness.
> Declaration of Independence

Let's go back over two hundred years to the summer of 1776, in Philadelphia, Pennsylvania. It was a difficult and dangerous time, especially for the men who made up the Continental Congress. For they were debating whether or not to break away from England. On June 7, 1776, Richard Henry Lee of Virginia introduced a resolution to Congress:

That these United Colonies are, and of right ought to be, free and independent States, they are absolved from all allegiance to the British Crown, and that all political connection between them and the state of Great Britain is, and ought to be totally dissolved.

To see how this had come about, let's go back a few more years. The British had been enacting laws that many colonists felt were unfair. For example, the colonists were allowed to sell their products only to Britain. But they wanted to sell their goods to any country that would pay a good price. Also, the British forced the colonies to import manufactured goods from England. The colonists wanted to manufacture their own goods.

In 1763 a law was passed that said colonists could not settle "on land beyond the beginning of the rivers that flowed to the Atlantic." The British felt that it cost too much to protect the settlers against the Indians. The colonists were furious, because they wanted the freedom to keep moving west.

Then followed many new tax laws enacted by Britain in which the colonists had no say. Many colonists felt that the British were getting rich by taxing them. "Taxation without representation is tyranny," they said.

Although many people did not want to pay these taxes, they had to, because British troops came to enforce the laws. And the colonists had to shelter and feed these soldiers!

A group of men began to write and speak out about independence. Some of these patriots were George Washington, a plantation owner; two lawyers, Thomas Jefferson and Patrick Henry; Benjamin Franklin, a printer and publisher; Paul Revere, a silversmith; and John Hancock, a businessman.

Fights began to break out between the British troops and the colonists. American towns formed groups of minutemen, volunteer soldiers ready to fight at a moment's notice. Finally, in April 1775, British and American soldiers clashed for the first time at the battles of Lexington and Concord in Massachusetts. The American Revolution had begun.

After nearly a year of war, Richard Henry Lee brought his resolution for independence before the Continental Congress on June 7, 1776, and again on June 10. But only eight of the thirteen colonies approved. The men knew that they needed to be strong and united against Britain. They needed the approval of all of the colonies. It was agreed to resume the debate on July 1.

On July 2, the colonies finally approved by a vote of 12 to 0 Lee's resolution for independence (New York chose not to vote). In the meantime, five men, Thomas Jefferson, John Adams, Benjamin Franklin, Robert R. Livingston, and Roger Sherman, had been appointed to write a declaration of independence. Because he was a talented writer, Thomas Jefferson was chosen to compose the first draft. In a rented room on Market and Seventh streets in Philadelphia, Jefferson worked for about two and a half weeks writing one of the most important documents in American history.

On June 28, Jefferson presented his draft to the Continental Congress. There were many arguments and debates over the exact wording of the document. Some changes were made. The men disagreed over a passage that condemned slavery. Finally, they decided to take this part out.

On July 4, 1776, a vote was taken. Nine colonies voted in

The historic signing of the
Declaration of Independence, July 4, 1776

favor of the Declaration of Independence, and John Hancock signed it to make it official. A printer worked through the night making handbills of the Declaration, which were passed out to the public the next day. The first newspaper to print the Declaration of Independence was the *Pennsylvania Evening Post*, on July 6, 1776. The news quickly spread to the other colonies.

At noon on July 8, the Declaration was read to the public for the first time in Independence Square in Philadelphia, and later that day in the center of town. Bonfires were lit to celebrate. Church bells rang out all day and night, including the great bell on top of the State House, later known as the Liberty Bell.

On July 9, the Declaration was read to George Washington's army in City Hall Park in New York. On August 2, members of the Continental Congress began to sign an official copy of the Declaration of Independence printed on parchment (special paper made from the skin of a sheep or goat), but the signing wasn't completed until several weeks later. Signing this document was a very bold move. The patriots knew that if they lost the war against Britain, they would be put to death for rebellion against the king. The American troops were outnumbered by the British, four to one. They also were opposed by many Americans, called loyalists because they wanted to remain loyal to King George. As John Hancock signed the Declaration on August 2, he said, "We must all hang together." Clever Benjamin Franklin answered, "If we don't, we shall all hang separately."

Why was the Declaration of Independence so important? It declared our independence from Great Britain, of course. But more important, it stated that a government should rule according to the wishes of the citizens, and only with their consent. If a government failed to do this, the citizens had the right to revolt. This important idea is the cornerstone for democracy in the United States. It meant freedom for Americans. And it also inspired other countries around the world to strive for self-government.

Fourth of July celebrations became a tradition right from the start in the city where the Declaration of Independence was written. In 1777, Philadelphia's churches rang their bells all day on the Fourth of July. Cannons boomed, soldiers paraded, bonfires burned, fireworks lit the skies, and candles glowed in the windows of patriots. Washington's soldiers celebrated too, because they were holding up well against British troops. They got extra rum to drink that day.

In 1783, when the Revolutionary War ended, Boston had its first Fourth of July celebration. An important Independence Day tradition was begun—having a famous person give a patriotic speech. Dr. John Warren, whose brother had been killed early in the Revolutionary War, spoke about the great future of America.

After the war, many soldiers moved west to Ohio, Kentucky, and beyond the Mississippi River. They loved their new country deeply, and they took with them the tradition of observing the Fourth of July with patriotic speeches and ceremonies.

When the Constitution was ratified in Philadelphia in 1788, the town went wild on the Fourth of July. Philadelphia was the capital of the United States then, and so there were many government officials to march in the parade, which lasted over three hours! Afterwards there were picnic lunches and patriotic speeches.

By the early 1800s, the Fourth of July was celebrated in

many places all across the country in much the same way: parades, patriotic speeches, bell ringing, displays of the flag, salutes at forts and on man-of-war ships, picnics, games, and, of course, fireworks.

Our bicentennial—the United States' 200th birthday—in 1976 was very grand indeed. Cities and towns all across the country restored historic buildings and districts and held patriotic festivals and exhibits. In New York City millions of people watched 212 sailing ships from thirty-four nations parade up the Hudson River. President Gerald Ford was aboard the aircraft carrier *U.S.S. Forrestal*. He rang the ship's bell thirteen times at 2:00 P.M. in honor of the original thirteen colonies. At the same time in Philadelphia, descendants of the men who signed the Declaration of Independence tapped gently on the Liberty Bell with a rubber mallet. (It is cracked and too fragile to be rung.) Bells all over the United States rang loud and clear. In Washington, D.C., that evening, two million people celebrated by watching 33 tons of fireworks explode in a fabulous display near the Washington Monument.

Today, towns and regions around the country have their own unique traditions that make Independence Day special.

In White Springs, Florida, the Old Fashioned Fourth of July Celebrations at the Stephen Foster Folk Culture Center include a special tribute to Stephen Foster, the famous composer of some of America's most popular songs. You've probably heard "Camptown Races" or "Swanee River" or some of his other songs.

There is an All Indian Pow Wow over the Fourth of July weekend in Flagstaff, Arizona. More than twenty tribes gather for ceremonies, tribal dances, and a rodeo.

*Vietnamese refugee children
practicing for their first Fourth of July
parade in the United States*

Eskimos hold their annual games in Kotzebue, Alaska, north of the Arctic Circle, on July 4. There are kayak races and beluga whale-watching contests.

In Lititz, Pennsylvania, people come from miles around to see the Festival of Candles. Homemade candles are arranged in the shapes of wheels, crescents, stars, and pyramids in Lititz Spring Park on the evening of July 4. A Queen of the Candles is chosen, and the candles are lit, turning the park into a wonderland of light.

Bristol, Rhode Island, hosts a Fireman's Muster on the Fourth. Fire engine companies from all over New England enter a water-squirting contest to see who can shoot streams of water from their hoses the farthest and highest.

Happy Birthday, America!!!

LABOR DAY

On the first Monday in September we honor those who work by giving them a day off! Labor Day is a day to commemorate our nation's work force. It was first observed on September 5, 1882, due to the efforts of Peter J. McGuire.

Mr. McGuire was a member of the Knights of Labor and the president and founder of the United Brotherhood of Carpenters and Joiners of America, an important labor union. Labor unions had been created to help the hundreds of thousands of factory workers gain fair wages and safe, satisfactory working conditions. Peter McGuire was a leader in the labor union movement. He suggested to the Central Labor Union of New York City that a day be spent honoring America's work force. So, on September 5, 1882, there was a huge Labor Day Parade and celebration in New York. Over ten thousand workers paraded, and there were dances, picnics, fireworks and speeches.

The General Assembly of the Knights of Labor passed a resolution in 1884 declaring the first Monday in September Labor Day and asking that it be an annual celebration. In 1887, Oregon became the first state to make Labor Day a state holiday. Thirty states observed Labor Day by 1893. And on June 28, 1894, President Grover Cleveland signed a bill passed by Congress that made Labor Day a legal holiday in the District of Columbia.

Today all fifty states celebrate Labor Day. The holiday has taken on a somewhat different meaning than it had a hundred years ago. Then, relations between workers and managers were often bitter. Workers were paid very low wages and forced to work in dirty, unsafe buildings. Some had to work long hours—twelve to fourteen hours a day, seven days a week.

Labor unions helped to improve working conditions, and Labor Day helped the country to recognize the hard work of men and women in factories everywhere. Today, of course, most workers enjoy fair wages and pleasant working conditions. Although still a day to honor labor with parades and speeches, Labor Day today is also the last summer fling before school begins. It's a day to spend with your family and friends taking that last weekend trip or having one more picnic before summer's end.

INAUGURATION DAY

Once every four years Washington, D.C., observes its own legal holiday—Inauguration Day—to allow the newly elected president and vice-president to take office. In 1933, the Twentieth Amendment to the Constitution set aside January 20 as the day that this would occur. Previously, Inauguration Day had been on March 4.

Children at a Labor Day powwow listen enthusiastically to a Shinnecock Indian. The annual weekend celebration in New York draws Indian tribes from all over the country.

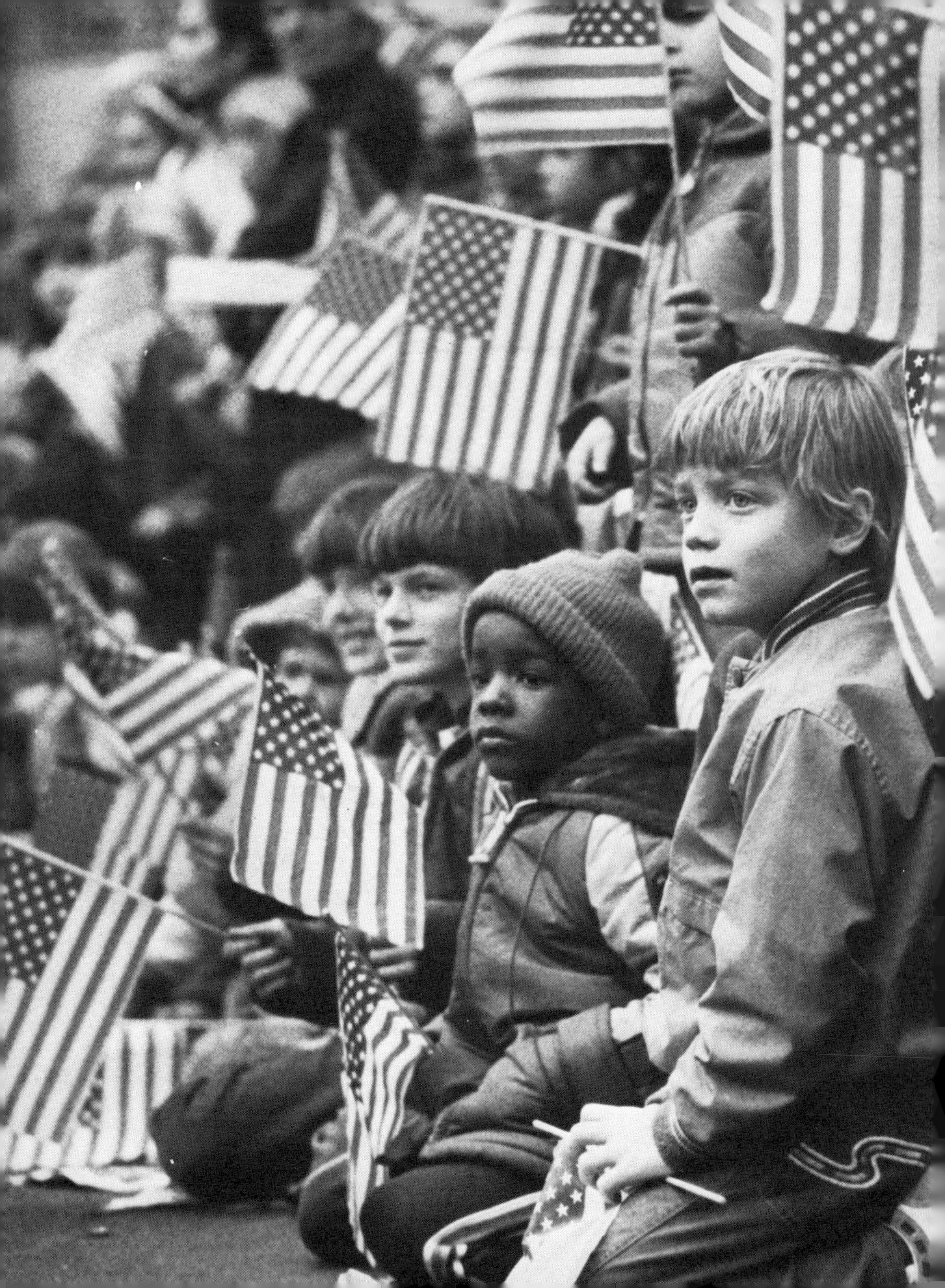

In many ways, Inauguration Day is always the same. Millions of visitors and television viewers watch the solemn ceremony that is held on a platform in front of the Capitol. There, every new president places his hand on the Bible and recites the following oath:

I do solemnly swear that I will faithfully execute the office of President of the United States, and will, to the best of my ability, preserve, protect, and defend the Constitution of the United States.

He then gives a speech and afterward watches a magnificent parade with marching bands and all branches of the military. An inaugural ball that evening ends the ceremonies.

Each Inauguration Day is unique, too, because each president is different. The first inaugural ceremony was very simple yet very dignified, because George Washington was a simple but dignified man. He rode in a coach drawn by six white horses to his inauguration, which took place in New York City on April 30, 1789. Because it was the first such ceremony, officials had to decide many things. For example, how should the new president be addressed? Some suggested that Washington be called "Your Highness." Others thought "Your Patriotic Majesty" was proper. Finally, it was decided to call him "Mr. President."

Andrew Jackson's Inauguration Day was very different from George Washington's. Mr. Jackson was well liked by the "common man"—the workers and small farmers of

Intently watching the Inaugural Parade in Washington, D.C.

America, rather than the wealthy landowners and businessmen. His inaugural ball was attended by men dressed in muddy boots and carrying pistols. The guests were rough and rowdy. They pushed and shoved, spilled lemonade and broke glasses. There were so many people at the ball that children were hurt and women fainted.

Abraham Lincoln's second inauguration was almost as wild as Andrew Jackson's. People were so eager to have a souvenir of the event they actually cut off pieces of the curtains in the ballroom to take with them! Guests couldn't wait to eat, and the floor became slippery with spilled food as they rushed to get their share.

John F. Kennedy's inauguration in 1961 was one of the grandest ever. It lasted for three days. Over 150 artists, authors, and musicians were among the guests invited to attend. A national symphony concert, a show performed by Hollywood stars, five balls, and numerous other events rounded out the festivities.

One of the saddest of all inaugurations was that of Lyndon Baines Johnson in 1963. President Kennedy had just been killed by an assassin. While the nation was still in shock, Johnson took the oath of office on a plane in Dallas which held the coffin of John F. Kennedy.

In 1985 Ronald Reagan was sworn into office for his second term. It was the fifiteth presidential inauguration in our country, and the four days of festivities included fireworks and a gala staged by movie stars.

PAN AMERICAN DAY

On April 14, some schools hold special activities to observe Pan American Day. There may be shows featuring music and dances with a Latin beat, skits, colorful posters, exhibits, and handicraft displays, and the good foods of our Latin American friends.

A man named James G. Blaine helped to foster our friendship with Latin America. As secretary of state under President Benjamin Harrison, he was known as the Father of Pan Americanism. In 1889, he called for an international conference that brought together the countries of North and South America. On April 14, 1890, delegates from these countries formed the Pan American Union, in which to promote international friendship and cooperation.

President Herbert Hoover declared April 14 as Pan American Day in 1931, and the twenty-one representatives have been celebrating it ever since. Today the Pan American Union is known as the Organization of American States (O.A.S.). Its purpose is to keep peace among its members and try to solve their problems. The O.A.S. includes South America, Central America, Mexico, and the United States.

Our Latin American neighbors are descendants of native Indians and Spanish, Portuguese, French, and black settlers. They speak Spanish, Portuguese, and French. Their governments are called republics, which means that they elect their rulers. However, many Latin American countries have had one revolution after another. Sometimes, even though the people elect a president, a dictator may take over. This has happened in some Latin American countries partly because there are a few wealthy, powerful landowners and many poor people. Unfortunately, due to these and other problems, the relations between some Latin American countries and the United States are not the best. A day like Pan American Day is very important because it gives us an opportunity to increase our understanding and respect for one another.

FLAG DAY

On June 14, 1777, in Philadelphia, the newly formed Congress resolved:

> That the flag of the thirteen United States be thirteen stripes, alternate red and white; that the union be thirteen stars, white in a blue field, representing a new constellation.

George Washington described what the colors and the symbols on the new banner meant:

> We take the stars from heaven, the red from our mother country, separating it by white stripes, thus showing that we have separated from her, and the white stripes shall go down to posterity, representing liberty.

The colonies had many flags before this one was chosen. For example, in New England the Liberty Tree banner was flown, showing a green pine tree standing in a field of white, with the words "An Appeal to Heaven" printed on it. Culpeper County in Virginia had a flag that showed a coiled rattlesnake and the words "Don't Tread on Me."

A special committee appointed by the Continental Congress had created the new design for the nation's flag. Historians once believed that Betsy Ross sewed our nation's first official flag. It is now thought by many that she was one of several women who made samples of the new flag.

In any case, it was proposed that a new star and a new stripe be added to the flag each time a new state joined the Union. Little did the first patriots know that there would eventually be fifty states!

At first, new stars and stripes were added with every new state. But in 1818, President James Monroe signed a bill that declared the official nation's flag would again have only thirteen stripes and that a new star would be added on the Fourth of July after a new state became part of the Union.

Our national anthem, "The Star Spangled Banner," is devoted to our nation's flag. Francis Scott Key, the composer, was inspired to write the song when he saw our flag amid bombs and flames during our second war with Britain on September 14, 1814.

You might wonder how our Pledge of Allegiance to the flag came to be. It is believed that in 1892 a children's magazine called *The Youth's Companion* was sponsoring a rededication to Americanism. The plan was to raise the national flag in all public schools on Columbus Day. James B. Upham, head of *The Youth's Companion,* wanted a new flag salute. Some say that Upham himself wrote the first draft of the Pledge of Allegiance, while others claim it was a former minister, Francis Bellamy. Both men worked on the staff of the magazine. In 1939 it was decided by a panel selected by the United States Flag Association that Francis Bellamy was the author. This decision was accepted by the American Flag Committee.

In 1877, one hundred years after our flag was adopted, Congress declared that the flag should be flown over public buildings on June 14. In 1916 President Woodrow Wilson proclaimed that Flag Day be observed on June 14. On this day the flag is displayed on all public buildings, schools, businesses and many private homes.

There are many different rules to follow in handling and displaying our nation's flag, for it must be treated with care and respect. Here are some of those rules:

1. The flag should be flown only from sunrise to sunset on buildings and flagstaffs in the open.
2. The flag should be displayed on all state and national holidays and on historic and special occasions. If the nation is in mourning for the death of an important person, such as a president, the flag is flown at half-mast.
3. Flags should be raised quickly, but lowered ceremoniously.
4. Never allow the flag to touch the ground when it is being raised or lowered.
5. Never hang or stretch out the flag carelessly.
6. When the flag is displayed vertically or horizontally against a wall, the blue field should be uppermost and to the observer's left.

CITIZENSHIP DAY

Citizenship Day, which falls on September 17, is actually a combination of two holidays that no longer exist—Constitution Day and I Am an American Day.

Constitution Day was observed to commemorate the signing of the Constitution on September 17, 1787. George Washington had presided over the Constitutional Convention during that summer long ago. America was a brand-new country; it had just won its freedom from Britain. A constitution was needed.

For many days the men studied codes of law and other important documents that would help them write a good constitution. After four months of work, they had a final draft which delegates from every state signed. Benjamin Franklin, James Madison, and Alexander Hamilton were among the first to sign the original Constitution.

Then the Constitution had to be ratified (approved) by at least nine of the thirteen states. Delaware, Pennsylvania, New Jersey, Georgia, Connecticut, Massachusetts, Maryland, South Carolina, New Hampshire, Virginia, New York, North Carolina, and Rhode Island approved the Constitution in that order. It was declared officially in effect on the first Wednesday in March—March 4, 1789.

The men who wrote the Constitution made sure that it could not be changed easily. To change it, a person must get approval of three-fourths of the states. The Constitution has withstood the test of time. Only twenty-six additions, called amendments, have been made in over two hundred years, although over four thousand changes have been proposed! Some of the suggestions that never went very far include allowing the president to rule for the rest of his life, outlawing duels, and even doing away with the states by dividing the country into four sections!

As for I Am an American Day, the American Legion proposed at their convention in Boston in 1940 that foreigners who had just become American citizens be honored. The day was especially popular during the 1940s and early 1950s. In 1952, President Harry Truman signed a bill passed by Congress that united Constitution Day and I Am an American Day, creating Citizenship Day, which is now observed on the anniversary of the signing of our Constitution.

UNITED NATIONS DAY

United Nations Day is a day we share with 158 other nations. It has been observed on October 24 since 1948—three years after the United Nations was created.

President Franklin D. Roosevelt was one of the first people to call for a worldwide organization for peace. The idea came about when he and representatives of twenty-five other nations met to try to make plans for winning World War II. Never again did they want to see such a terrible war. So, after it was over, delegates from fifty nations met in San Francisco. President Harry Truman was our country's representative because Roosevelt had died.

There they wrote the Charter of the United Nations, which, among other things, proposed to save the world from war and safeguard basic human rights. Any peace-loving and self-governing nation was free to join the United Nations.

In 1945 the United Nations Charter was approved. The first United Nations Day was celebrated in 1948. Today, as on that first day, the United Nations holds public rallies, panel discussions, and seminars. Speeches are given and many information centers are open to the public. All of this takes place in the beautiful United Nations building on the East River in New York City.

It is there that the U.N. holds meetings of the Security Council and the General Assembly, the two main parts of the organization.

The Security Council has five permanent members: England, the Soviet Union, China, France, and the United States. There are six other member nations that are temporary. Each of the permanent members has veto power. If one votes no, the plan being considered is not carried out. The Security Council's main purpose is to preserve peace throughout the world. When possible, it sends U.N. peacekeeping soldiers where they are needed.

The General Assembly is made up of every nation that belongs to the U.N. Each nation has one vote. The General

*Celebrating United Nations Day,
children from around the world gather
in the playground of the
United Nations International School.*

Assembly meets in September, October, and November of each year.

GENERAL ELECTION DAY

When you reach the age of eighteen, if you are a United States citizen, you will be able to vote. You might be surprised to learn that only about half of the people who are eligible to vote in our country actually do.

When our country was first formed, people took voting more seriously. About 80 percent of the men who could vote did so in the early days. Yes, men—for women and many others could not vote. Before everyone could vote, we had to add three amendments to the Constitution and enact some new laws. The Fourteenth Amendment defines American citizenship. The Fifteenth Amendment says that someone cannot be prevented from voting because of race, color, or "previous condition of servitude." The Nineteenth Amendment, ratified in 1920, gives women the right to vote.

In some parts of the country, poll taxes (fees) were charged to those who wanted to vote. Sometimes people had to pass reading and writing tests before they could vote. These were tactics used to try to deny blacks the right to vote. Since many blacks were poor and uneducated, many could not vote. The Twenty-fourth Amendment, ratified in 1964, eliminated poll taxes in federal elections. And the Voting Rights Bill, passed in 1965, forbade literacy tests.

The last group to gain the right to vote were the American Indians. By 1948 every state allowed Indians to vote.

In 1845, the first Tuesday after the first Monday in November was set aside by Congress for presidential elections. These occur every four years, counting from the first year in the century. In most states, General Election Day is a legal holiday.

Congressional elections are also held on the first Tuesday after the first Monday in November. Members of the House of Representatives are elected every two years and senators are elected every six years. Maine is the only state that differs. Congressional representatives in Maine are elected on the second Monday in September.

Each state sets its own dates for state elections, as do towns and cities.

BILL OF RIGHTS DAY

After the Constitution was written and ratified, the lawmakers of newly formed America knew that their work was not yet over. Many felt that the Constitution was not enough. They wanted the rights of American citizens to be written out and added to the Constitution. So, the Bill of Rights was created.

On September 25, 1789, President James Monroe introduced twelve constitutional amendments to the first Congress. There was heated debate, and finally they were approved. After over two years, the required two-thirds of the states ratified ten of the amendments on December 15, 1791. Two were discarded.

These ten amendments guarantee the rights of free people, protecting them from tyrannical government. The amendments include:

1. Freedom of religion, speech, press, assembly, and petition.
2. The right to keep and bear arms.

3. Rights regarding the housing of soldiers.
4. Rules about the government's right to search and seizure.
5. Protection of people and their property.
6. The rights of those accused of a crime.
7. The right to a trial by jury.
8. Protection against excessive fines, bail, and punishment.
9. A guarantee of unspecified rights.
10. Powers reserved to the states and to the people.

In 1941, on the 150th anniversary of the ratification of the Bill of Rights, President Franklin D. Roosevelt proclaimed December 15 as Bill of Rights Day. He urged citizens to display the American flag on that day.

Many schools put on plays and pageants to observe Bill of Rights Day, and newspapers often sponsor essay contests for students.

ACTIVITIES

Summer Shindig
Have an old-fashioned picnic for the Fourth of July or Labor Day. Play some of the games that pioneer children used to enjoy long ago:

Corn-shucking contest:
Divide your friends into teams, giving each team the same number of ears of corn. See who can shuck their share the fastest. Afterwards, enjoy eating the fruits of your labor!
Watermelon spitting:
When you get to dessert, see who can shoot their watermelon seeds the farthest.

After dinner:

You can play football like New England pioneers used to do. Kick the ball around instead of carrying it, sort of like soccer. And the goals are much farther apart than in a football field. One goal might be a grove of trees, the other goal a far hilltop.

Another popular game was torpedoes. Each player is given six chestnuts or buckeyes. The object is to get your torpedo into the hat or basket placed 1 to 2 feet (.3 to .6 m) from a wall, by aiming the buckeye or chestnut so it will hit the wall and fall into the basket. Award one point for each basket.

Don't forget tug-of-war and sack races for lots of laughs.

Start a Collection

Perhaps you'd like a hobby that's patriotic in nature that you can enjoy all year. You could collect patriotic buttons or stamps. Each year there are new stamps and buttons issued, so you'll be kept busy for a lifetime adding to your collections. Buttons are popular during presidential campaigns. Stamps come in beautiful series that reflect our nation's history and achievements.

Another satisfying hobby is building and collecting model cars, boats, trains, and airplanes. There are thousands of models on the market to choose from. Start off easy and work toward more complicated pieces. You can specialize if you like, and collect only aircraft from World War I, or famous aircraft carriers, or old-model trains. It's up to you and your imagination.

2

PEOPLE AND PERSONALITIES

Three people—George Washington, Abraham Lincoln, and Christopher Columbus—are honored with days of their own. A fourth person, Martin Luther King, Jr., will be honored with a national holiday beginning in 1986. In this section, we'll take a look at these important people, plus other well-known figures you might want to commemorate with special events.

PRESIDENTS' DAY

George Washington and Abraham Lincoln were two of our greatest and best-loved presidents. We observe the birthdays of both. Washington's Birthday falls on February 22 and Lincoln's on February 12. Many states now observe one holiday, the third Monday in February, and call it Presidents' Day.

GEORGE WASHINGTON'S BIRTHDAY

Numerous legends have grown over the years about the Father of our country. Parson Mason Locke Weems wrote many tales about George Washington. The most famous tells of how George, as a young boy, chopped down his father's cherry tree. When his father asked who chopped down the tree, George is said to have replied, "I cannot tell a lie. I did cut it with my hatchet."

Historians now doubt that such stories by the Parson Weems actually happened, but they do reveal that Washington was a person of honor and integrity.

We do know that Washington was born on February 22, 1732, on a plantation in Virginia. When he was eleven, his father died, and George went to live on his older brother's plantation, Mount Vernon.

As a young man, Washington was a surveyor, measuring and mapping the land, and an officer in the colony of Virginia's army. After leading Virginia's troops in the French and Indian War, Washington married Martha Custis, a widow with two children, and went to live with his new family at Mount Vernon.

When the colonists declared their independence from Britain, Washington was asked to become commander in chief of the colonial army. He accepted the job reluctantly. His was a ragtag army, far outnumbered by the British. He set about training the assortment of men and boys who made up his army. There was never enough food, clothes, equipment, or ammunition. Often, the soldiers suffered from cold and frostbite. The winter of 1778 at Valley Forge, Pennsylvania, was the most terrible time of all. Many of the soldiers had no shoes, and instead wore bloody rags. But there was hope, too. For Washington was a strong, inspiring leader. His soldiers were devoted to him. On his birthday, they played the fife and drums for him. And that winter the soldiers were trained by Baron von Steuben, a former Prussian officer. It was a turning point in the war. The soldiers gained strength and military expertise and eventually began to win the war. The British finally surrendered at Yorktown, Virginia, on October 19, 1781.

This famous painting depicts Washington, commander of the American army during the Revolutionary War, leading his men across the Delaware River.

Washington was devoted to his army, and he cried when he said good-bye to them. But he looked forward to retiring to Mount Vernon and plantation life.

That was not to be. He was elected first president of the United States. Washington served two terms; he declined to serve a third term. Finally, he was able to retire to Mount Vernon.

Washington's last birthday was on the wedding of his granddaughter, Nelly Custis. The wedding took place at Mount Vernon in 1799. Washington wore his old uniform from the Revolutionary War, but the day was a far cry from the bleak birthday he celebrated with his troops that winter of 1778. Washington died on December 14, 1799.

Washington's Birthday has been celebrated in various ways around the country ever since his death. Nowadays, schools, banks, libraries, and government offices are closed. There is a wreath-laying at his burial site in Mount Vernon, which is beautifully preserved and attracts thousands of visitors each year. At Valley Forge, Pennsylvania, there is a re-enactment of the military exercises Washington and his soldiers performed.

The Washington Memorial in Washington, D.C., is a beautiful tribute to his memory. Dedicated in 1885, the Memorial overlooks Alexandria, Virginia, where Washington went to church, and the Potomac River, where he swam as a boy.

ABRAHAM LINCOLN'S BIRTHDAY

Just nine years after Washington's death, the man was born who helped save our country when it was being torn apart by civil war. Abraham Lincoln was born on February 12,

1809, in a tiny log cabin at Hodgenville (Hardin County), Kentucky. He went to school for only one year, but he loved to read and that is how he got his education.

He was a tall, thin, and rather awkward man who was uncomfortable in high society, but who made friends easily and loved to tell jokes. He often wore a tall, black hat, called a stovepipe hat, where he kept letters and notes tucked away in the inside band.

During the time that Lincoln was making a name for himself in politics, the North and the South were disagreeing over the issue of slavery. Most Southern plantation owners had slaves, cheap labor that they needed to help raise cotton. In return, plantation owners took care of the slaves and gave them shelter. The North, which was mainly industrial, did not need slave labor. Northerners were against owning and selling slaves. Lincoln hated slavery, and the South knew it. When he was elected president of the United States in 1861, eleven Southern states separated from the nation. The Civil War began on April 12, 1861.

In 1862, Lincoln issued the famous Emancipation Proclamation, which declared that after January 1, 1863, all slaves in the part of the country under Confederate control would be free. The Thirteenth Amendment, ratified two years later, made slavery illegal everywhere in the United States.

The Civil War was a tragic, bloody war that ended after four years on April 9, 1865. After the South surrendered, Lincoln looked forward to rebuilding the nation. He had led the North to victory and he had helped to free the slaves.

Abraham Lincoln

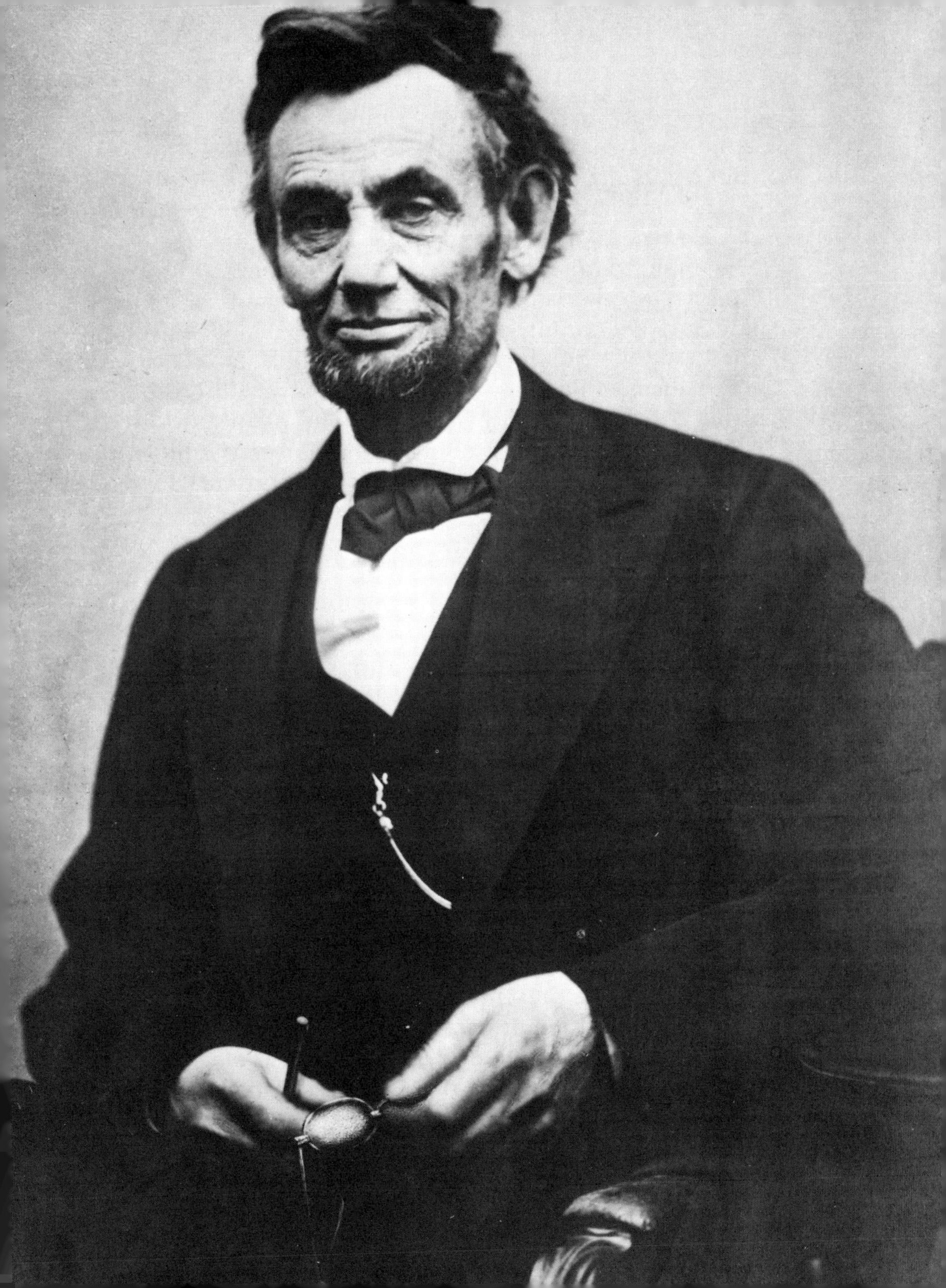

Now he wanted to help heal the wounds between the North and the South.

But it was not to be. Only five days after the South surrendered, on April 14, 1865, Lincoln was shot and killed by an actor named John Wilkes Booth.

Beginning with the first year after Lincoln's death, his birthday was celebrated in many different kinds of gatherings across the country. In 1892, Illinois made Lincoln's birthday a state holiday, and many other states followed. Today, Lincoln's Birthday is observed along with Washington's on the third Monday in February in many states.

Abraham Lincoln has a fine memorial in Washington, D.C. Dedicated in 1922, it is a grand sculpture of Lincoln, seated, that faces the Washington Monument.

MARTIN LUTHER KING, JR., DAY

A new national holiday was recently created by Congress and President Ronald Reagan. In 1986 on the third Monday in January, Martin Luther King, Jr., Day will be celebrated as an official national holiday for the first time. During his lifetime, King worked to help blacks, the poor, and the disadvantaged gain equal rights.

Congress had debated the issue of whether to declare King's birthday a national holiday for fifteen years. Finally, on October 19, 1983, the Senate voted 78 to 22 to pass the bill. Well-known blacks, including Coretta Scott King (King's widow), and singer Stevie Wonder, who wrote a song for the King holiday, were present for the vote.

Martin Luther King, Jr., was born on January 15, 1929, in Atlanta, Georgia. As a young boy, he saw that blacks in the South were denied many of the rights that whites enjoyed.

He and other blacks were victims of segregation: blacks were forced to go to schools that were inferior to the schools that whites attended. Blacks had to give their bus seats to whites. Blacks could not drink out of the same water fountains as whites or use the same rest rooms.

Even more important, blacks were often forced to take literacy tests or pay special fees before they could vote. They were not hired for good jobs or given the same opportunities as whites.

King knew that education was important. He got a bachelor's degree in sociology. Then he studied to become a minister and went on to get his Ph.D.

In 1954 he took a job as a pastor for the Dexter Avenue Baptist Church in Montgomery, Alabama. By the next year he would become the leader of the civil rights movement in the United States. It all started when Rosa Parks, a black Montgomery citizen, refused to give her bus seat to a white person. She was arrested. In protest, blacks and whites, led by King, did not ride the city buses until the law was changed. It took a year of boycotting the buses to get the law changed.

King went on to become the president of the Southern Christian Leadership Conference (SCLC), which helped to work toward desegregation and civil rights. He was deeply influenced by the writings of Mohandas K. Gandhi, an Indian leader who had helped India achieve independence from Britain just after World War II. Gandhi believed that nonviolent protest and civil disobedience were effective ways to change unjust laws.

Martin Luther King led others in such nonviolent protests to get the laws changed for the better. He staged marches, boycotts, and protests, and tried to keep them nonviolent. Many times, however, fighting broke out between police and protestors. Once, King's home was bombed. Another time, a church was bombed and young children were killed.

King helped to organize and lead the historic March on Washington on August 28, 1963. Thousands of blacks and whites marched to Washington to demonstrate their desire for full civil rights. King gave a speech entitled "I Have a Dream" that will never be forgotten by those who heard it.

In 1963, *Time* magazine chose King to be man of the year. In 1964 he was awarded the Nobel Peace Prize. He was the youngest man ever to receive it.

Partly due to King's efforts, the Voting Rights Act, which forbade requiring voters to take literacy tests, was passed in 1965.

King's life came to a tragic end. On April 4, 1968, he was shot and killed outside of his hotel room in Memphis, Tennessee.

Martin Luther King's work was not finished. His widow, Coretta Scott King, and many other civil rights leaders carry on his work today, hoping to achieve fuller citizenship rights for blacks and other minority groups.

Many schools throughout the country have observed King's birthday since his death. Beginning in 1986, our nation will be united in observing this day to honor one of our greatest leaders.

COLUMBUS DAY

One of the greatest adventures of all time was Christopher Columbus's discovery of America. It came about after many years of hoping and effort by Columbus.

Christopher Columbus was born during the fifteenth century in Genoa, Italy. Growing up along the Mediterra-

Martin Luther King, Jr., leading the crowd at the historic March on Washington civil rights rally

nean seacoast, Christopher grew to love the sea. By the time he was sixteen, he knew how to navigate a sailing vessel and had taken a voyage to Iceland.

He moved to Portugal, a great seafaring nation, and became a master map maker. At that time, some well-educated people believed that the world was round, and Christopher Columbus was one of them. He wanted a chance to sail straight into the horizon and prove his theory. He believed that he would not fall off the edge of the world, as most people feared, but that he would come back to his starting point.

The king of Portugal refused to sponsor such a trip, so Columbus turned to Queen Isabella and King Ferdinand of Spain. After many years, they finally agreed. Spain was eager to find new routes to India to bring back silks, perfumes, spices, and other goods, which at that time had to be carried by camel through the desert past hostile Turks.

Columbus was given three ships, the *Niña*, the *Pinta*, and the *Santa Maria*, plus enough money to pay a crew for four months. Crew, officers of the king, doctors, and servants were among the 90 men who were to set sail. Four of the passengers were prisoners who had been sentenced to death. They were offered their freedom in return for sailing with Columbus.

They set sail on August 3, 1492. A typical day on the long journey consisted of morning prayers, singing songs while working on deck, and evening prayers. The men let their beards grow long and went barefoot. They had wine and fresh water to drink, plus meat, biscuits, and occasionally cheese, onions, and other vegetables to eat.

The journey was dangerous and frightening. One of the first things to go wrong was that the *Pinta*'s helm was broken when they reached the Canary Islands. It took one month to repair the ship. Then, just after setting sail again, they hit a calm that kept them in one spot for two days. Not even a tiny breeze blew. The crew thought it was a bad omen.

Finally, trade winds began to blow, and the three ships sailed for ten days. But many of the crew became frightened because there was no sign of land. They begged to be allowed to turn back. Some of them planned to mutiny, or rebel against their leaders.

September 18 was the last day of good sailing weather. The winds turned against them, and they sailed only 380 miles (610 km) in six days. The crew was about to form a rebellion, but Columbus knew they were close to spotting land. On September 21 they had seen seaweed and large clumps of land covered with vegetation. Then, flocks of birds were seen flying southwest, so Columbus changed course slightly to follow them.

Columbus promised money and a fine silk doublet to the first person to see land. On October 11, the crew of the *Niña* discovered a green branch, a flower, and a carved stick floating in the water.

Finally, it happened. At 2:00 that following morning, October 12, someone on the *Pinta* shouted, "Tierra, tierra!" ("Land, land!"). At daybreak they landed.

Columbus had arrived at what is now known as the Bahamas. He thought he had reached India. The crew saw natives, "Indians," that they found very strange. They were covered with grease and paint and were wearing no clothes!

For ten days Columbus and his men explored the islands. Then the *Niña* traveled back to Spain with the *Pinta*. The *Santa Maria* had sunk on a reef. Columbus came home to a welcoming parade and dancing in the streets. He had brought with him six native Indians, plus parrots and other animals from the New World.

In 1934, President Franklin D. Roosevelt issued a proclamation asking that October 12 be observed as a national holiday. Columbus Day is a holiday in most states and in Puerto Rico. And it is a holiday that we share with Central and South American countries, some parts of Canada, Italy, and Spain.

Look for an especially important Columbus Day in 1992—it will be the 500th anniversary of Columbus's voyage!

ACTIVITY

Remembering Others
Robert E. Lee faced the most difficult decision of his life. The South, his home, had broken away from the United States over the issue of slavery. It was civil war. Abraham Lincoln had asked Lee to command the Union Army. Should he fight on the side of the North? He felt that slavery was wrong, but he also felt that the federal government was violating the Constitution by forcing the South to end slavery. Lee chose to leave the U.S. Army, in which he had been an officer for thirty years, and to lead the army of Virginia instead.

Lee and the South were defeated, of course. When he surrendered, Lee told his soldiers to become loyal U.S. citizens once again. Today many Southern states remember their great leader on his birthday, January 19. To celebrate Lee's birthday, you could re-enact this important turning point in his life. Write your own script and select members of your class to play the parts.

A portrait of Christopher Columbus

Choose your favorite character from American history, and celebrate his birthday by re-enacting a scene from his life. For example, Thomas Jefferson is an interesting figure. His birthday is on April 13. You could show him presenting the first draft of the Declaration of Independence to the Continental Congress.

Other possibilities are Susan B. Anthony, whose birthday is on February 15, or Elizabeth Cady Stanton, who was born on November 12. During the 1800s both of these women worked to gain equal rights for women, including the right to vote. Go to the library and find out what turning points in their lives would make interesting plays.

Franklin D. Roosevelt is another interesting possibility. One of our greatest presidents, he led us through the Great Depression and World War II. On his birthday, January 30, you could stage a play showing what he did to help put people back to work or how he made plans to fight World War II.

America has many more, important people from its past and also contributing today. Part of the fun is choosing your favorite person. The possibilities are endless!

3
MILITARY HOLIDAYS

D-Day, June 6, 1944, was the famous invasion of American, British, and Canadian troops against the Germans on the coast of France. It marked the beginning of the end of World War II. Many soldiers died in this invasion. In 1984, thousands of veterans, along with kings, queens, presidents, and prime ministers, went to France for D-Day's fortieth anniversary. Jet fighters left plumes of red, white, and blue smoke in the sky as an aircraft carrier and seven warships sailed below. A special ceremony on land included speeches by President Reagan and French President Mitterrand.

Some of the most important patriotic holidays are days such as this one in which we remember soldiers who died defending our country in past wars, those who survived, and those who stand ready to defend our country today. We will take a look at two very important military holidays that are observed without fail every year—Memorial Day and Veterans' Day. We'll also look at Armed Forces Day, which is observed with special events in Washington, D.C., and at military bases.

MEMORIAL DAY

Memorial Day, 1984, was a very special Memorial Day indeed. For on that day, the Unknown Serviceman of Vietnam was laid to rest in the Tomb of the Unknowns in Arlington, Virginia.

The body of the Unknown Serviceman had lain in state in the Capitol in Washington, D.C., for three days. Then it was brought to Arlington, where, in a special ceremony, President Reagan bestowed upon it the Medal of Honor. There was a twenty-one-gun salute, soldiers fired three volleys, and a bugler played "Taps." The Serviceman was then buried next to three other unknown soldiers—one each from World War I, World War II, and the Korean War. It was a sad moment, a time to remember. Many Vietnam veterans and families of veterans stood by and watched, moved to tears.

The Vietnam War had ended eleven years before, but it had taken a long time for an unknown soldier to be found. The Unknown Serviceman was the *only* American soldier who could not be identified out of the 58,012 killed.

Memorial Day is a day to honor and remember the soldiers who have died defending our country in U.S. wars. It is celebrated as a legal holiday on either May 30 or the last Monday in May in Washington, D.C., Puerto Rico, the Northern states, and many Southern states. In the South, many states also observe Confederate Memorial Day to honor the soldiers who fought in the Confederate Army during the Civil War. (To learn more about Confederate Memorial Day, turn to page 58.)

No one is sure exactly how Memorial Day got started. The people of Boalsburg, Pennsylvania, believe that their town was the birthplace of Memorial Day. There, a Miss Emma Hunter decided to decorate her father's tomb with flowers in 1864. He had been a colonel and had fought in the Battle of Gettysburg in the Civil War. While in the graveyard, Miss Hunter met a woman whose son had been killed in the war.

These two women decided to meet the next year to decorate the graves.

Memorial Day was probably a tradition that started in the South and spread to the North. Just after the Civil War, some Confederate women decided to decorate the graves of soldiers. On April 26, 1886, they put magnolia blossoms on both Confederate and Union soldiers' graves. Word of this reached the North and the story was printed in the *New York Herald Tribune*.

The Grand Army of the Republic—the Union veterans' organization—and its commander in chief, John A. Logan, were the first to call for May 30 as a day to decorate the graves of those who died to preserve the unity of our country in the Civil War. Logan's wife had traveled to the South and had seen Confederate graves decorated with flowers, wreaths, and flags. She suggested that the North do the same to honor their soldiers.

Adjutant General N.P. Chapman of the Grand Army also claimed the credit for having originated Memorial Day. A soldier had told him that in his native country of Germany it was customary to place flowers on the graves of loved ones in the spring.

In any case, the Grand Army organized the first Memorial Day observance in 1868 at the National Cemetery in Arlington, and several other communities across the country joined in. Slowly, the day began to be observed all across the country. In 1873, New York became the first state to make it a legal holiday. Now, the day is set by a presidential proclamation. At first, it was called Decoration Day, but the name Memorial Day gradually became accepted, and it is intended to honor all American soldiers who had lost their lives in any war in which the United States took part.

Today, in towns all across the country, there are parades, speeches, and ceremonies to remember the dead soldiers. Flags fly at half-mast and families remember loved ones killed in the Vietnam, Korean, and two World Wars. While towns and cities remember their veterans, a grand military ceremony takes place in Arlington National Cemetery, where row upon row of white gravestones mark the graves of thousands of fallen soldiers. In recent years, Memorial Day has been especially meaningful to the thousands who lost friends and family members in the Vietnam War. They travel from all parts of the country to see the Tomb of the Unknowns and the recently erected Vietnam War Memorial, which contains the names of all but one of the 58,012 Americans who died in Vietnam.

VETERANS' DAY

Veterans' Day, which falls on November 11, has been observed for many years, but before 1954 it was called Armistice Day. The first Armistice Day was November 11, 1918, and it was the day that the peace treaty was signed by Germany and the Allies, ending World War I. (An armistice is a truce or cease-fire just before the signing of a peace treaty.) It had been a long and bloody war. More soldiers had died in World War I than in any other war in history. On that first Armistice Day, journalist George Honey, an Australian, called for two minutes of silence as the peace treaty was signed. Even radio broadcasts came to a halt at 11:00 A.M. on that day as people remembered the many fallen soldiers.

Honey had started a tradition called the "Great Silence" that is observed even today at the hour when fighting

Soldiers celebrating the end of World War I

stopped in World War I. In addition to this "Great Silence," numerous communities across the country hold parades of veterans from World War II, the Korean War, and the Vietnam War. The American flag is flown in public places and private homes. You will notice blue and gold stars in the windows of many houses. These stars are symbols of soldiers who fought in a war. A blue star means that the soldier in the particular family is living, and a gold star means that the soldier died.

A veteran may step up to you and ask if you want to buy an artificial poppy. These little red flowers are also sold on Memorial Day. They are symbols of the soldiers who have not died in vain. The money raised from selling these poppies is used to help wounded war veterans.

A very solemn ceremony takes place at Arlington National Cemetery in Virginia, where the president and others lay a wreath on the Tomb of the Unknown Soldiers. This tomb first came to be in 1921, when an unidentified soldier was chosen to represent all of those who had died in World War I. The body lay in state in Washington, D.C., for three days in November. Thousands of people passed by to say a prayer and honor the war dead. On November 11 at 11:00 A.M., it was lowered into the tomb, on which were the words:

> *Here rests in honored glory*
> *An American Soldier*
> *Known but to God.*

Today, of course, there are four soldiers in the Tomb of the Unknowns—one each from World Wars I and II, the Korean War, and the Vietnam War.

Armistice Day had been created by presidential proclamation in 1919. In 1927, Congress passed a resolution calling for the flag to be displayed in public places on November 11. People were asked to observe the day in schools and churches.

In 1938, Congress passed a bill that November 11 should be known as Armistice Day. That year, President Franklin D. Roosevelt signed a bill making the day a legal holiday in the District of Columbia.

But World War II was just around the corner. As the world again went to war, Americans lost interest in Armistice Day. After the war, veterans wanted November 11 to be a day honoring soldiers of *all* wars in which Americans fought, not just World War I.

Emporia, Kansas, went down in history as the first place to hold a Veterans' Day rather than an Armistice Day, on November 11, 1953. Representative Edward J. Rees introduced a bill in the House of Representatives that would change Armistice Day to Veterans' Day. The bill passed, and Mr. Rees wrote to all state governors for approval of Veterans' Day as a state holiday.

By an act of Congress on May 24, 1954 and signed into law on June 1, 1954 by President Eisenhower, Armistice Day was officially changed to Veterans' Day. It is a legal holiday in all states except Oklahoma, where observance is optional, Washington, D.C., and Puerto Rico.

ARMED FORCES DAY

The day that we honor our armed forces—the Navy, the Air Force, the Army, and the Marines—was set aside as a special day by presidential proclamation in 1947, the year that our government's Department of Defense was created. To some degree, it replaced Army, Air Force, and Navy Days which were once observed. Throughout the years, our government has believed that by maintaining a strong military, we can help to keep peace in the world. The third Saturday in May, Armed Forces Day, is the time we pay tribute to the men and women who protect our country.

If you live near a military base, you can see Armed Forces Day observed in all its splendor. For example, at Andrews Air Force Base in Camp Springs, Maryland, there is a Joint Services Open House. There are air shows by the U.S. Navy's Blue Angels, the U.S. Army's Golden Knights, and other air squads, plus displays of defense equipment.

Armed Forces Day is your opportunity as a civilian to visit military bases and observe special programs put on by the Navy, Air Force, Army, and Marines. You may see exhibits and demonstrations of new weapons or jet fighter planes and helicopters. You may be able to board a naval vessel or take a tour of a military base. And you can talk with officers, soldiers, sailors, and pilots. If you are thinking of joining the military someday, Armed Forces Day is a good time to learn about military life and the responsibilities and challenges that go along with it.

ACTIVITIES

1. Veterans and soldiers always have interesting stories to tell. Have everyone in your class write down an interesting tale told by a relative or older friend who fought in World War II, the Korean War, or the Vietnam War. You may even know someone who is presently in the military or stationed overseas. Collect all of these tales and make a book of war stories.

2. To go with your book, have your classmates bring in souvenirs or mementos from relatives' war days. You can set up

an interesting exhibit on Veterans' Day or Memorial Day that may include old helmets, uniforms, canteens, and medals. Be sure to get permission before you bring these items to school—and handle them with care! Old objects are valuable and are treasured by their owners.

4
SOME REGIONAL HOLIDAYS AND CELEBRATIONS

Every region and state has its own special days in which to celebrate its heritage. Some of these events draw a few thousand people. Others draw hundreds of thousands of visitors. It's impossible to include every single such holiday in the country. Here is just a sample.

ARBOR DAY

A people without children would face a hopeless future; a country without trees is almost as hopeless.

Theodore Roosevelt

When J. Sterling Morton, a journalist, moved to the Nebraska Territory from Detroit in 1854, he found that his new home was a bare plain, with not a tree in sight. He missed the trees he had enjoyed in Michigan. He knew that settlers in Nebraska needed trees as protection from the severe blizzards of the Great Plains. And they needed trees to keep the soil from blowing away, to provide shade and fruit, and to make the landscape more beautiful.

In his newspaper, Sterling Morton wrote about the importance of trees. He encouraged homesteaders to plant trees on their land. In 1872, he convinced Nebraska's board of agriculture to declare April 10 a special day for planting trees. Morton's home, Arbor Lodge, had been planted with many different kinds of trees, and the day for tree planting was named Arbor Day after his home. A million trees were planted in Nebraska on that first Arbor Day!

Every state in our country observed Arbor Day by 1894. But, each state celebrates Arbor Day on a different day—usually sometime in the spring, whenever is best for planting in that part of the country. National Arbor Day falls on the last Friday in April. But schools and communities usually observe Arbor Day whenever their state does.

Schoolchildren across the country have been especially active on Arbor Day. Most Arbor Day activities consist of a retelling of the history of Arbor Day, songs and poems about trees—and, of course, tree planting, both at home and in the community. Arbor Day 1980 was especially meaningful in Grand Island, Nebraska, where a tornado had struck. A concerned citizen bought six thousand trees that were planted by schoolchildren. Each child was given three seedlings on Arbor Day—a silver maple, a green ash, and a hackberry. The kids planted them at home and at school, to replace the trees that had been lost. And they even went to school all summer long to water their trees!

Cities can be made more beautiful with trees, too. The city of Winchester, Virginia, has a "Shade for Today" program. A resident there can have a tree planted on the parkway in front of his or her home for thirty-five dollars.

You can raise money for a good cause and have trees planted in your community at the same time. Just write to the National Arbor Day Foundation, 100 Arbor Avenue, Nebraska City, Nebraska 68410. Through their tree sales program you can sell red maple, sugar maple, redbud, tulip tree, purple leaf plum, pin oak, black walnut, and hazelnut trees. You will make a profit of $1.25 for each tree that you sell. The Arbor Day Foundation will tell you which trees will grow best in your state. And don't worry if you don't know much about tree planting; they supply complete and easy instructions.

Another idea is to make up your own unique Arbor Day celebration at school. Write to the National Arbor Day Foundation (address above) for more ideas and for their newsletter.

SAINT PAUL WINTER CARNIVAL

It all started in 1885 when a New York newspaperman wrote that St. Paul, Minnesota, was "another Siberia, unfit for human habitation in winter."

This statement made the people who lived in St. Paul angry. They decided to prove that the city was a delightful place to live in the wintertime. The Saint Paul Winter Carnival Association was formed to plan an annual winter carnival.

A gigantic palace made of ice was erected in the town's Central Park. A large toboggan course was built. And for ten days the townspeople celebrated. There were all kinds of winter sports, such as skating, skiing, and horse racing. There were masked balls and parades. The first Saint Paul Winter Carnival was a huge success.

A "legend" grew about the winter carnival, known as the Legend of Boreas. It told of how Boreas, or the North Wind, proclaimed the carnival to celebrate the winter paradise of Saint Paul. This angered Vulcanus, the God of Fire, and set off the annual struggle between the forces of nature, between winter and spring.

Today, the Saint Paul Winter Carnival is one of the largest festivals in the nation. It is held from the last weekend in January through the first weekend in February. There is no longer an ice castle built each year, for that is too expensive. But the Queen of the Snows is chosen and crowned. There is ski jumping, tobogganing, skating, parades, and pageants. The National Outdoor Speed Skating Championships are part of the Carnival, as are the National Majorette Championships, Ice Capades, sports car racing on ice, an ice fishing contest, and a huge square dance festival.

PATRIOTS' DAY

At midnight on April 18, 1775, General Thomas Gage, the royal governor of Massachusetts, sent eight hundred of his men to seize military supplies that the rebel colonists had stockpiled in Concord, Massachusetts. But that night, Paul Revere rode through the streets shouting a warning and calling the colonists to action. When the British reached Lexington, only 6 miles (10 km) from Concord, they found seventy-seven armed farmers waiting for them in the dawn light.

There on the village green on April 19, 1775, the American Revolution began. The colonists refused to put down their arms at the order of Major Pitcairn, and the battle was on. Several colonists and British soldiers were killed; some were wounded. The tiny American army, called the minutemen, retreated. There was another battle when the British reached Concord, and both sides lost men.

Massachusetts celebrated Patriots' Day for the first time in 1894. Today, Patriots' Day is celebrated on the third Mon-

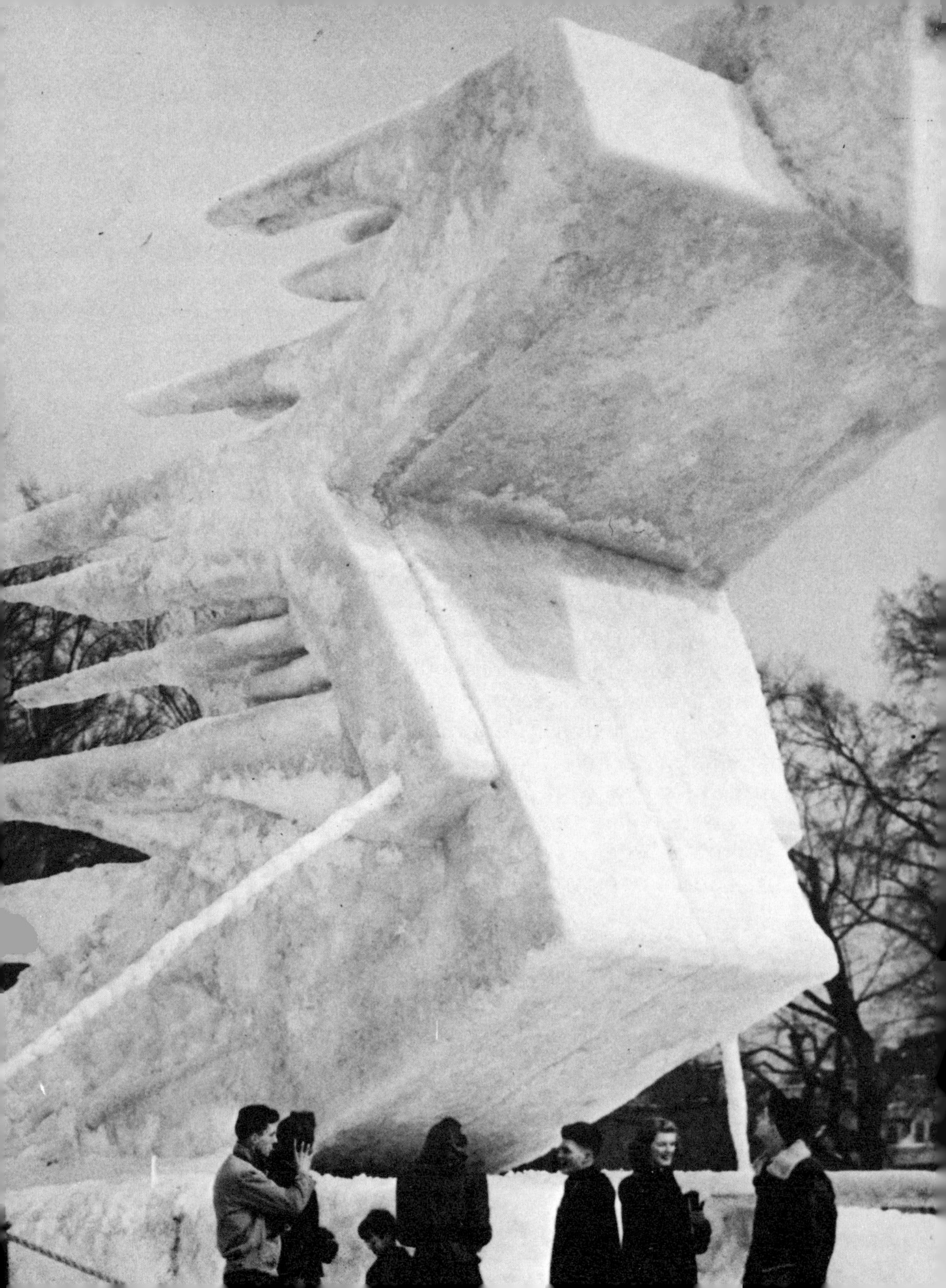

Left: *a large eagle ice sculpture, the patriotic theme of a winter carnival in the Northeast.* Above: *a Patriots' Day parade in Boston*

day in April. A legal holiday in Massachusetts and Maine, Patriots' Day commemorates the battles of Lexington and Concord of 1775. The Massachusetts cities of Arlington, Boston, Brookline, Cambridge, Concord, Lexington, Medford, and Somerville stage elaborate re-enactments of the battles and Paul Revere's ride, in addition to parades and other festivals.

A monument stands at the Old North Bridge near Lexington and Concord, inscribed with the famous lines of poetry by Ralph Waldo Emerson:

> Here once the embattled farmers stood
> And fired the shot heard round the world.

CONFEDERATE MEMORIAL DAY

Memorial Day actually began, it is believed by many, in the South, and later caught on in the North. To this day, the Southern states have a special Confederate Memorial Day Celebration in addition to the Memorial Day observed by most of the nation.

Mrs. Elizabeth Rutherford Ellis of Columbus, Georgia, is thought to have begun the Confederate Memorial Day tradition. She was a member of the Ladies' Aid Society, an organization of women active during the Civil War. The women sewed for the soldiers and visited patients in a local hospital. They decorated the graves of soldiers who died in the hospital with flowers and plants. Mrs. Ellis (then Miss Rutherford) had heard of the German custom of caring for the graves of dead heroes, and she suggested that a special day be set aside for this purpose in the South to honor the fallen Confederate soldiers.

Miss Rutherford proposed that April 26 should be the day, because it was the date that Confederate general Joseph E. Johnston surrendered at Greensboro, North Carolina. Thus, the first Memorial Day ceremonies were held on April 26, 1865 in a Columbus, Georgia, cemetery.

The first official observance of Memorial Day took place April 26, 1866, at Columbus, Georgia. Today "Yankees" of the North celebrate Memorial Day and in Dixie (the South) special ceremonies remember the brave Confederate heroes of the South.

CINCO DE MAYO

Cinco de Mayo means 5th of May in Spanish. And that is a very special day indeed for Mexicans, Mexican Americans, and other Americans, too. In 1862 on that day in Puebla, Mexico, the tiny, outnumbered Mexican army defeated the French army of Napoleon III which was planning to capture Mexico City and the whole country.

Ever since that day, no foreign power has ever invaded North America. In Mexico, Cinco de Mayo is a national holiday. In our country, Cinco de Mayo is observed wherever there are large populations of Mexican Americans, such as California, Texas, and New Mexico.

Schoolchildren especially like to celebrate this day—it is one giant fiesta, with music, singing, dancing, eating, and playing. You're likely to see more people wearing colorful Mexican dress and sombreros than traditional American clothing. Mariachis (roving musicians) stroll city streets and parks playing guitars, violins, and trumpets. The aroma of tortillas (flat pancakes filled with beans, lettuce, tomatoes, and, sometimes, hot sauce) and other good Mexican food fills the air.

Schools hang the green, red, and white Mexican flag. There are all kinds of Mexican games to play, taco eating contests, etc. Classes make special exhibits, booths, and murals. And at night, the piñata—a sort of clay pot decorated with bright tissue paper and hung from the ceiling—is struck until it is broken, releasing candy for everyone!

CHEYENNE FRONTIER DAYS

If you want to see the biggest outdoor rodeo in the world, Cheyenne Frontier Days in Cheyenne, Wyoming, is the place to go! Every year for nine days in July, over twelve hundred riders, ropers, and doggers compete for more than $400,000 in prize money. Here you will see saddle bronc riding, bareback riding, bull riding, calf and steer roping, and steer wrestling. The world's best cowboy will be named and awarded a trophy buckle studded with diamonds.

After you've learned all about rodeos, there are still chuckwagon, quarterhorse, and wild horse races to see. And if you get tired of rodeos and races, there is square dancing, country music, four parades, an open house at F. E. Warren Air Force Base, a show by the USAF Thunderbirds Aerial Demonstration Team, a carnival, a chili cook-off, free pancake breakfasts, and dancing by the Southern Plain Indians.

AMERICAN INDIAN DAY

The history of the true native Americans, the Indians, is a sad one.

At first, Indians and white settlers from Europe were friendly with each other, although rather wary because each found the other's customs strange. But the Indians helped the Pilgrims through their first rugged winter in America by showing them how to plant corn and hunt.

Eventually, however, as more new settlers came to America, the Indians realized that their land was being taken. Fighting began to break out between pioneers and Indians. Sometimes bands of Indians attacked white settlements or wagon trains. Time and again, white settlers made treaties with the Indians, promising not to trespass on Indian land, but time after time the treaties were broken. The Indians were slowly pushed farther and farther west.

Not only were Indians losing their land, but they were also losing their source of food and hides, for the buffalo was quickly being killed off by white settlers.

By 1887, all of the Indians surrendered to the Americans. They were forced to move to reservations set aside by the government in Oklahoma, Arizona, and Utah. Life on these reservations was hard. The Indians' old way of life was gone forever, and they had to adapt to the poor living conditions on the reservations.

Things finally began to change in the early 1900s, when Americans began to realize the terrible injustice they had done to the Indians. In 1924 all American Indians were declared citizens of the United States. This gave them the right to vote in elections and made them eligible for government aid. In 1947 the Indian Claims Commission was set up to investigate the many claims of Indians who had been cheated out of land. Many Indians were paid for the land that had been taken from them.

Gradually, we have learned to appreciate Indian customs and traditions. Today, many people enjoy Indian music, art, tribal rituals, and poetry.

American Indian Day was created to recognize the role that Indians played in American history. It is celebrated on the fourth Friday in September in some states. The first major observance of the day occurred on the second Saturday in May, 1916, in New York State, a land of numerous Indian reservations.

Friday, September 23 was proclaimed American Indian Day by Governor Rockefeller of New York in 1960, to honor the state's Indians. Today, the day is observed in several states by governor's proclamation or legislation. Some states observe it on the second Saturday in May, others on the fourth Friday in September; still others have different dates.

ACTIVITY

Your Own Patriotic Holiday
Declare your own patriotic holiday. With the help of your classmates, find out about the history of your town, city, or state. Visit the library and local historical societies and museums for ideas. Write to your local or state chamber of commerce to find out what is celebrated in your area.

Set aside a special day for celebrating your holiday. You could stage a play about interesting events from the history of your region. Ask local historians or museum officials to speak about your local heritage. Have exhibits of old photographs and drawings of the way your town used to look. Invite local craftspeople to demonstrate their skills. Happy celebrating!

PATRIOTISM ALL YEAR ROUND

MARTIN LUTHER KING, JR., DAY
Third Monday in January (beginning 1986)

ROBERT E. LEE'S BIRTHDAY
January 19 or Third Monday in January

INAUGURATION DAY
January 20

FRANKLIN D. ROOSEVELT DAY
January 30

SUSAN B. ANTHONY DAY
February 15

PRESIDENTS' DAY
Third Monday in February

THOMAS JEFFERSON'S BIRTHDAY
April 13

PAN AMERICAN DAY
April 14

ARMED FORCES DAY
Third Saturday in May

MEMORIAL DAY
May 30

FLAG DAY
June 14

INDEPENDENCE DAY
July 4

LABOR DAY
First Monday in September

CITIZENSHIP DAY
September 17

COLUMBUS DAY
October 12

UNITED NATIONS DAY
October 24

GENERAL ELECTION DAY
First Tuesday after First Monday in November

VETERANS' DAY
November 11

ELIZABETH CADY STANTON DAY
November 12

BILL OF RIGHTS DAY
December 15

INDEX

Italicized page numbers indicate photographs.

Activities, suggested, 26–27, 40, 42, 50–51, 62
Adams, John, 5
American Indian Day, 60–62
American Revolution, 4–5, 7–8, 29, 55, 58
Anthony, Susan B., 42
Arbor Day, 52–54
Armed Forces Day, 49–50
Armistice Day. *See* Veterans' Day

Bellamy, Francis, 19
Bill of Rights Day, 25–26
Blaine, James G., 17

Calendar of holidays and celebrations, 63–64
Chapman, N. P., 45
Cheyenne Frontier Days, 60
Cinco de Mayo (5th of May), 59–60
Citizenship Day, 20–21
Civil rights movement, 34–36
Civil War, 31, 32, 40, 58–59
Cleveland, Grover, 12
Columbus, Christopher, 28, 36, 38–40, *41*
Columbus Day, 19, 36, 40
Confederate Memorial Day, 44, 58–59

Custis, Martha, 29

Declaration of Independence, 3–5, *6*, 7–8
D-Day, 43
Decoration Day. *See* Memorial Day

Eisenhower, Dwight D., 49
Ellis, Elizabeth Rutherford, 58
Emerson, Ralph Waldo, 58

Ferdinand, King, 38
Flag Day, 18–20
Ford, Gerald, 9
Forrestal, U.S.S., 9
Foster, Stephen, 9
Fourth of July. *See* Independence Day
Franklin, Benjamin, 5, 7, 20

Gage, Thomas, 55
Gandhi, Mohandas K., 35
General Election Day, 24–25
George III, King, 3
Hamilton, Alexander, 20
Hancock, John, 5, 7
Harrison, Benjamin, 17
Henry, Patrick, 5
Honey, George, 46
Hoover, Herbert, 17
Hunter, Emma, 44

]65[

Inauguration Day, 12, *14*, 15–16
Independence Day, 3, 8–9, *10*, 11
Isabella, Queen, 38

Jackson, Andrew, 15–16
Jefferson, Thomas, 5, 42
Johnson, Lyndon B., 16
Johnston, Joseph E., 59

Kennedy, John F., 16
Key, Francis Scott, 19
King, Coretta Scott, 34, 36
King, Martin Luther, Jr., 28, 34–36, 37
Korean conflict, 48

Labor Day, 11–12, *13*
Lee, Richard Henry, 4, 5
Lee, Robert E., 40
Lincoln, Abraham, 16, 28, 31–32, *33*, 34
Lincoln's Birthday, 31–34
Livingston, Robert R., 5
Logan, John A., 45

McGuire, Peter J., 11
Madison, James, 20
Martin Luther King, Jr., Day, 34, 36
Memorial Day, 43–46
Mitterrand, François, 43
Monroe, James, 19, 25
Morton, J. Sterling, 52

Napoleon III, Emperor, 59
National Arbor Day Foundation, 53, 54
New York Herald Tribune, 45

Pan American Day, 16–17

Parks, Rosa, 35
Patriots' Day, 55, *57*, 58
Pennsylvania Evening Post, 7
Presidents' Day, 28

Reagan, Ronald, 16, 34, 43, 44
Rees, Edward J., 49
Revere, Paul, 5, 55
Rockefeller, Nelson, 62
Roosevelt, Franklin D., 21–22, 26, 40, 42
Roosevelt, Theodore, 52
Ross, Betsy, 18

Saint Paul Winter Carnival, 54–55
Sherman, Roger, 5
Stanton, Elizabeth Cady, 42

Time, magazine, 36
Truman, Harry, 21, 22

United Nations Day, 21–22, *23*, 24
Upham, James B., 19

Veterans' Day, 46, *47*, 48–49
Vietnam conflict, 44, 48
Von Steuben, Baron, 29

Warren, John, 8
Washington, George, 5, 15, 18, 20, 28–29, *30*, 31
Washington's Birthday, 28, 31
Weems, Mason Locke, 28–29
Wilson, Woodrow, 19
World War I, 46, 47, 48
World War II, 22, 43, 48, 49

The Youth's Companion, magazine, 19